CHILDREN'S AUTHORS

RICK RIORDAN

Jill C. Wheeler
ABDO Publishing Company

visit us at
www.abdopublishing.com

Published by ABDO Publishing Company, PO Box 398166, Minneapolis, Minnesota 55439. Copyright © 2013 by Abdo Consulting Group, Inc. International copyrights reserved in all countries. No part of this book may be reproduced in any form without written permission from the publisher. The Checkerboard Library™ is a trademark and logo of ABDO Publishing Company.

Printed in the United States of America, North Mankato, Minnesota.
102012
012013

Cover Photo: Getty Images
Interior Photos: AP Images pp. 13, 19, 21; Getty Images pp. 5, 11; iStockphoto pp. 7, 9
Percy Jackson & the Olympians: The Lightning Thief by Rick Riordan. Copyright © 2005 by Rick Riordan. Reprinted by permission of Disney • Hyperion, an imprint of Disney Children's Book Group, LLC. All rights reserved. p. 15
Percy Jackson & the Olympians: The Demigod Files by Rick Riordan. Copyright © 2009 by Rick Riordan. Reprinted by permission of Disney • Hyperion, an imprint of Disney Children's Book Group, LLC. All rights reserved. p. 16
Percy Jackson & the Olympians: The Last Olympian by Rick Riordan. Copyright © 2009 by Rick Riordan. Reprinted by permission of Disney • Hyperion, an imprint of Disney Children's Book Group, LLC. All rights reserved. p. 17
The Kane Chronicles: The Red Pyramid by Rick Riordan. Copyright © 2010 by Rick Riordan. Reprinted by permission of Disney • Hyperion, an imprint of Disney Children's Book Group, LLC. All rights reserved. p. 18
From a cover of THE 39 CLUES: BOOK ONE - THE MAZE OF BONES by Rick Riordan Copyright © 2008 by Scholastic Inc. Reprinted by Permission
THE 39 CLUES is a registered trademark of Scholastic Inc. p. 20

Series Coordinator: Megan M. Gunderson / Editors: Tamara L. Britton, Stephanie Hedlund
Art Direction: Neil Klinepier

Cataloging-in-Publication Data

Wheeler, Jill C., 1964-
 Rick Riordan / Jill C. Wheeler.
  p. cm. -- (Children's authors)
Includes bibliographical references and index.
ISBN 978-1-61783-578-0
1. Riordan, Rick, 1964- --Juvenile literature. 2. Authors, American--20th century--Biography--Juvenile literature. 3. Children's stories--Authorship--Juvenile literature. I. Title.
813/.6-dc23
[B]
                                                                        2012946385

CONTENTS

Tales of Olympic Proportions

Rick Riordan (RYE-r-don) has always loved mythology. He has shared that love with millions of young readers through the Percy Jackson & the Olympians series. He has introduced readers to some terrific, and very old, stories.

Riordan's books were not overnight hits. They began with small **print runs**. Excited readers would pass the books along. Friends gave them to friends and parents gave them to children. Teachers passed them on to students. The books gained popularity over time.

Now, the Percy Jackson books have been translated into more than 30 languages. They have sold more than 15 million copies in the United States alone. Yet Riordan does not measure success by book sales. He is more interested in getting kids hooked on reading.

Riordan began his writing career creating award-winning mystery novels for adults. After starting a family, he began writing stories for young readers.

Recently, Riordan has been working on a **multimedia** project. It combines novels with online games and activities. He is excited about the potential of the Internet to get kids to read even more.

Hearing that kids became readers because of Percy Jackson is the best part of Riordan's job.

TEXAS TOT

Rick Riordan was born on June 5, 1964, in San Antonio, Texas. His parents were teachers. His mother taught high school art. His father was a **vocational** education teacher.

Growing up, Rick assumed he would be a teacher, too. In class, he sometimes thought about how he would explain things differently if he were the teacher. Rick was creative at home, too. He liked building things with Lego blocks, constructing robots, and creating imaginary worlds.

One thing young Rick did not enjoy was reading. He thought the books he was supposed to read in school were boring. He just didn't connect with them.

Things changed when Rick was around 12 years old. A series of good English teachers introduced him to fantasy stories and mythology. The first books he truly enjoyed reading were the Lord of the Rings **trilogy** by J.R.R. Tolkien. He also devoured Greek and Norse myths.

In eighth grade, Rick wrote a story of his own. His English teacher, Mrs. Pabst, read the story. She suggested he try to get it published. So, Rick sent the story to *Asimov's Science Fiction* magazine. Today, Rick still has the rejection letter he received. He even had it framed!

San Antonio, Texas

WANNABE MUSICIAN

Rick continued writing fantasy and science fiction while at Alamo Heights High School. He worked on the high school newspaper, too. In fact, he won a state award for feature writing.

Rick also wrote an **underground** newspaper poking fun at his high school. He once made the mistake of making fun of the school's losing football team. To get revenge, the players threw eggs at his car!

In addition to improving his writing skills, Rick explored a passion for music. He had dreams of making it big as a musician. He even grew long hair, a beard, and a mustache to look like a real rock star.

After high school, Rick entered North Texas State University in Denton to study guitar. He later transferred to the University of Texas at Austin (UT). To help pay for school, Rick played in **cover bands**. He also tried his hand at songwriting. Writing **lyrics** helped Rick learn what makes a good line of writing.

For three summers during college, Rick worked as music director at Camp Capers. Later, he would use his experience at this summer camp in a book.

The University of Texas at Austin

California Teacher

Riordan earned a double **major** in English and history from UT. By graduation, he had set aside dreams of working as a musician. He had decided to keep reading and talking about books.

Riordan wanted to get **certified** to teach English and history. So, he entered the University of Texas at San Antonio. As part of his training, he did his **student teaching** in San Antonio. After graduation, his first full-time teaching job was at a middle school in New Braunfels, Texas.

In 1990, Riordan moved to San Francisco, California, for a new job. He began teaching middle school English at Presidio Hill School. He and his wife, Becky, spent eight years in California. The area was beautiful. Yet Riordan found himself homesick for Texas.

To cope, Riordan began writing a detective novel called *Big Red Tequila*. The book features a private investigator named Tres Navarre. Riordan later said the book was a "love letter to San Antonio."

Riordan finished the book in 1994. After lots of rejection letters, the book was finally published in 1997. Six more Tres Navarre mysteries were published over the next ten years.

Riordan's interest in mysteries began in college.

BACK TO TEXAS

In 1998, the pull of Texas became too much for the Riordans. They returned to San Antonio. There, Riordan took a job at Saint Mary's Hall. He taught middle school English and social studies.

Riordan's students knew their teacher was also an author. He told them his novels were not appropriate for young people. But that did not stop his students from reading them! They often asked him why he did not write books for young people. Riordan never had a good answer to that question.

By this time, Riordan and his wife had two sons named Haley and Patrick. By the time Haley reached second grade, he was having trouble with reading and writing. The Riordans learned Haley had **dyslexia** and **ADHD**. Soon, this would change everything.

Having supportive, caring teachers inspired Riordan to become a writer and a teacher himself.

BEDTIME STORIES

Riordan and his wife went to work figuring out how to help their son. They realized that Haley had a strong interest in mythology. So, Riordan began sharing stories from Greek mythology with him at bedtime. Haley always wanted more. Eventually, Riordan ran out of stories!

That's when Riordan recalled a creative writing project he had given his students. The project asked each student to create a "demigod hero." This type of character is the son or daughter of a god. So, the character is partly a god, too. The student's task was to write a Greek-style quest for his or her character.

Riordan decided to do this project himself to help Haley. He began to spin Haley a special bedtime story. It was the tale of a boy who learns he is the son of **Poseidon**. The boy has to recover **Zeus**'s master lightning bolt from modern-day America. The character also happens to have **dyslexia** and **ADHD**.

It took many evenings of bedtime stories for Riordan to weave the tale of young Percy Jackson. When he was finished, Haley asked him to write down the story. Riordan did. The story formed the basis for Riordan's first book for kids, *The Lightning Thief*.

Fans of the Percy Jackson series love that it is inventive and action-packed!

A New Audience

It took time for Riordan's bedtime story to become a children's book. First of all, he was busy! Riordan still taught full-time. And, he was writing one Tres Navarre book a year.

Riordan was not sure he could take on more work. Yet Haley insisted he bring Percy Jackson to life to share with others.

So Riordan pressed on. It took him months to turn the story into a **manuscript**. Then, he shared it with his students. He was very nervous showing his work to sixth, seventh, and eighth graders.

Thankfully, the students loved the story. They also had some ideas for how to make it better. Riordan had called his manuscript "Son of the Sea God." His student critics thought that name gave

The Demigod Files includes three short stories about Percy Jackson.

away too much too quickly. Thanks to their feedback, Riordan found a better title.

Writing for a younger audience has helped Riordan become a better writer. He feels that adults will put up with information that does not directly relate to the story. Younger readers will not.

Riordan also believes young readers demand great characters, an engaging plot, humor, and very clear writing. That is exactly what he gave them with his Percy Jackson & the Olympians series.

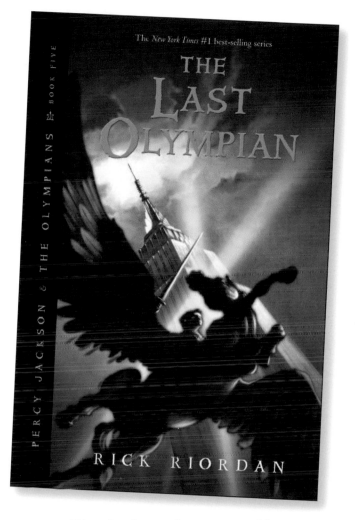

Riordan's students gave him feedback on how Percy's sword should work.

From Texas to Greece and Egypt

In 2002, Saint Mary's Hall honored Riordan with their first Master Teacher award. Two years later, Riordan made the difficult decision to quit teaching. That way, he could focus on writing. Riordan had always loved teaching. He just could not do both anymore.

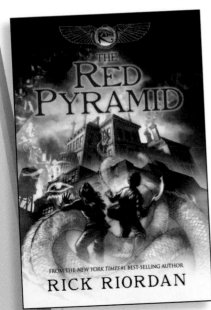

The Lightning Thief was published in 2005. Riordan followed it with five more Percy Jackson books. *The Sea of Monsters* was published in 2006, followed by *The Titan's Curse* in 2007. *The Battle of the Labyrinth* came out in 2008. Finally, *The Last Olympian* and *The Demigod Files* were published in 2009.

That same year, Riordan introduced two new series. In the Heroes of Olympus series, Riordan once again tells stories about demigods. The series features some characters from the Percy Jackson books. The Kane Chronicles series focuses on ancient Egypt. But it still has all the exciting mythology and magic of Riordan's other works!

In 2010, the movie version of **The Lightning Thief** *was released. Actor* **Logan Lerman** *brought Percy Jackson to life on screen.*

Multimedia Experiences

As the Percy Jackson series was wrapping up, Riordan took on a totally different project. In 2008, *The 39 Clues: The Maze of Bones* was published. In addition to the novel, the project included a Web site and trading cards. Riordan wrote the first novel. Then, other authors wrote the remaining books in the series.

When Riordan has spare time, he still enjoys reading. He also likes to swim, play guitar, and play

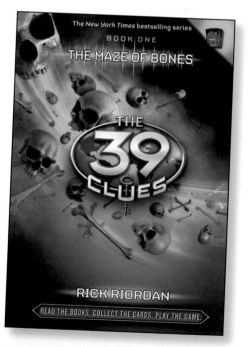

Riordan was unable to write all of the 39 Clues books. The publication schedule required publishing a new book every two to three months!

Riordan has traveled throughout the United States and Canada to promote his books.

video games with his sons. He enjoys traveling with his family as well.

Riordan misses teaching, but he still spends a lot of time in classrooms talking to students about writing. He jokes that now he has millions of kids in his classroom instead of 30. Even better, he does not have to grade any papers! Instead, he talks to young aspiring writers. He tells them to read a lot, write every day, and never get discouraged.

GLOSSARY

ADHD - attention deficit/hyperactivity disorder. A mental disorder involving restlessness and being unable to concentrate.

certified - to be recognized as having met certain requirements.

cover band - a band that plays music written and performed by another group. Often, the music was made famous by a more popular band.

dyslexia (dihs-LEK-see-uh) - a condition in the brain that makes it hard for a person to read, write, or spell.

lyrics (LIHR-ihks) - the words of a song.

major - a particular subject or field of study.

manuscript - a handwritten or typed book or article not yet published.

multimedia - using or involving more than one type of medium, such as television and the Internet.

Poseidon - in Greek mythology, the god of the sea. He carries a trident and drives a horse-drawn chariot. Poseidon is a brother of Zeus, king of the gods.

print run - a batch of copies of a book printed at one time.

student teaching - practice teaching a student does while studying to be a teacher. He or she is supervised by an experienced teacher.

trilogy - a series of three novels, movies, or other works that are closely related and involve the same characters or themes.

underground - existing outside of an established group or organization.

vocational - relating to training in a skill or trade to be pursued as a career.

Zeus - in Greek mythology, the king of the gods. He rules from Mount Olympus. Zeus is known as the god of rain, wind, thunder, and lightning. He is often shown holding a thunderbolt.

To learn more about Rick Riordan, visit ABDO Publishing Company online. Web sites about Rick Riordan are featured on our Book Links page. These links are routinely monitored and updated to provide the most current information available.

www.abdopublishing.com

INDEX